What Happens at a Magazine?/
¿Qué pasa en la editorial de una revista?

By/por Lisa M. Guidone

Reading Consultant: Susan Nations, M.Ed.,
author/literacy coach/consultant in literacy development/

Consultora de lectura: Susan Nations, M.Ed.,
autora/tutora de alfabetización/consultora de desarrollo de lectoescritura

WEEKLY READER®
PUBLISHING

Please visit our web site at www.garethstevens.com. For a free catalog describing
Gareth Stevens Publishing's list of high-quality books, call 1-800-542-2595 (USA) or
1-800-387-3178 (Canada). Our fax: 877-542-2596

Library of Congress Cataloging-in-Publication Data

Guidone, Lisa M.
      [What happens at a magazine? Spanish & English]
      What happens at a magazine? / by Lisa M. Guidone ; reading consultant,
      Susan Nations = Qué pasa en la editorial de una revista? / por Lisa M. Guidone ;
      consultora de lectura, Susan Nations.
          p. cm. — (Where people work = Dónde trabaja la gente?)
      Includes bibliographical references and index.
      ISBN-10: 0-8368-9281-X   ISBN-13: 978-0-8368-9281-9 (lib. bdg.)
      ISBN-10: 0-8368-9380-8   ISBN-13: 978-0-8368-9380-9 (softcover)
      1. Periodicals—Juvenile literature. I. Nations, Susan. II. Title.
  III. Title: Qué pasa en la editorial de una revista?
  PN4832.G85   2009b
  050—dc22   2008014484

This edition first published in 2009 by
Weekly Reader® Books
An Imprint of Gareth Stevens Publishing
1 Reader's Digest Road
Pleasantville, NY 10570-7000 USA

Buddy® is a registered trademark of Weekly Reader Corporation. Used under license.

Senior Managing Editor: Lisa M. Herrington
Creative Director: Lisa Donovan
Designer: Alexandria Davis
Translation: Tatiana Acosta and Guillermo Gutiérrez

Photo Credits: All photographs by John Klein except page 13 courtesy of Sean Parkes
and page 19 courtesy of Rudy Sigrist.

The publisher thanks Linda Ruggieri, Jeff Talbot, Rachelle Kreisman, Charlene Pinckney, Kevin Lui,
and Sean Parkes for their participation in this book. Special thanks also goes to Quebecor World in
Cincinnati, Ohio, and Nancy Barron and Becky Tanner at the Burnham School in Bridgewater, Connecticut.

Printed in the United States of America

1 2 3 4 5 6 7 8 9 10 09 08

Hi, Kids!

I'm Buddy, your Weekly Reader® pal. Have you ever visited a magazine? I'm here to show and tell what happens at my magazine—*Weekly Reader*. So, come on. Turn the page and read along!

— — — — — — — — —

¡Hola, chicos!

Soy Buddy, su amigo de Weekly Reader®. ¿Han visitado alguna vez la editorial de una revista? Estoy aquí para contarles lo que pasa en la editorial de mi revista: *Weekly Reader.* Así que vengan conmigo. ¡Pasen la página y vamos a leer!

Boldface words appear in the glossary.

— — — — — — —

Las palabras en **negrita** aparecen en el glosario.

How is a magazine made? It starts with a great idea! Many people make *Weekly Reader*. They meet to plan the topic. This magazine will be about frogs. Ribbit, ribbit!

– – – – – – – – –

¿Cómo se hace una revista? ¡Todo empieza con una buena idea! Muchas personas participan en la publicación de *Weekly Reader*. Primero, estas personas se reúnen para decidir el tema. Este número tratará sobre las ranas. ¡Croac, croac!

A writer looks up facts about frogs. Then it is time to write. She writes many **drafts**. Each draft makes the writing better.

– – – – – – – – – –

Una escritora busca información sobre las ranas. Después, se pone a escribir. Escribe muchos **borradores**. En cada uno, va mejorando el texto.

writer/
escritora

Next, the story goes to the **editor**. The editor makes sure the story is clear. She checks that the sentences and the words are right.

— — — — — — — — — —

Después, el artículo pasa a la **editora**. Ésta se asegura de que la información se entiende. Comprueba que las oraciones y las palabras están escritas correctamente.

editor/
editora

9

Now it's time to find the photos. There are lots of cover photos! Which one will be chosen?

- - - - - - - - - -

Ahora es el momento de buscar las fotografías. ¡Hay muchas fotos para la portada! ¿Cuál será la elegida?

**cover photos/
fotografías para la portada**

An **artist** draws my picture for the magazine. Don't I look cute?

— — — — — — — — — —

Un **artista** dibuja mi personaje para la revista. ¿No les parezco adorable?

artist/
artista

13

A **designer** comes up with the look of the magazine. He puts the words and pictures together on pages.

– – – – – – – – – –

Un **diseñador** decide qué aspecto tendrá la revista. Organiza el texto y las imágenes en las páginas.

designer/
diseñador

15

Many people look at the pages called **proofs**. A **proofreader** reads the proofs for mistakes.

– – – – – – – – – –

Varias personas revisan las páginas, que ahora se llaman **pruebas**. Un **corrector de pruebas** las lee por si hay errores.

proofs/
pruebas

proofreader/
corrector de pruebas

Now the magazine goes to the printer. The magazines come off a noisy printing press. Trucks bring them to schools across the country.

— — — — — — — — —

Ahora, la revista se envía a la imprenta. Los ejemplares van saliendo de una ruidosa prensa. Unos camiones los llevan a escuelas de todo el país.

printing press/
prensa

19

Hop to it! Kids in class are ready to learn about frogs.

— — — — — — — — —

¡Ábrela de un salto! Los niños de esta clase están listos para aprender cosas de las ranas.

21

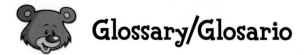

Glossary/Glosario

artist: a person who draws or paints pictures

designer: a person who puts words and photos together on a page

drafts: early writings from which a final story is made

editor: a person who checks a story to make sure that the writing is clear and that there are no mistakes

proofreader: a person who reads over pages and fixes mistakes

proofs: the pages of a magazine or a book before it is printed

— — — — — — — — —

artista: persona que hace dibujos

borradores: escritos iniciales de donde sale un artículo

corrector de pruebas: persona que lee las páginas para buscar y corregir los errores

diseñador: persona que organiza el texto y las imágenes en una página

editor: persona que revisa un artículo para asegurarse de que el texto se entiende y de que no hay errores

pruebas: páginas de una revista o un libro antes de que se impriman

For More Information/Más información

Books/Libros

Magazines. John Hamilton
(ABDO Publishing Company, 2004)

What Do Authors Do? Eileen Christelow
(Clarion Books, 1997)

What Do Illustrators Do? Eileen Christelow
(Clarion Books, 2007)

Web Site/Página web
Weekly Reader
www.weeklyreader.com
Write to Buddy and find games, activities, and more!/
¡Escríbanle a Buddy y encuentren juegos, actividades y más!

Index/Índice

About the Author

Lisa M. Guidone works in children's publishing. She has written and edited children's books and magazines for Weekly Reader for nearly eight years. She lives in Trumbull, Connecticut, with her husband, Ryan. She dedicates this book to her new nephew, Anthony, in hopes he shares her love of reading.

Información sobre la autora

Lisa M. Guidone trabaja haciendo libros para niños. Durante casi ocho años ha escrito y corregido libros y revistas infantiles para Weekly Reader. Lisa vive en Trumbull, Connecticut, con su esposo Ryan. Este libro se lo dedica a su nuevo sobrino, Anthony, con la esperanza de que comparta con ella el amor por la lectura.